# QUEEN MARY'S DOLLS' HOUSE

## ON A SCALE OF ONE TO TWELVE

### OFFICIAL GUIDE

### KEY TO PLAN

1. Princess Royal's Room
2. Sitting Room
3. Night Nursery
4. Maid's Room
5. King's Bedroom
6. King's Bathroom
7. Garage
8. Library
9. Day Nursery
10. Queen's Bedroom
11. Kitchen
12. Wine Cellar
13. Linen Room
14. Housekeeper's Room
15. Saloon
16. Strong Room
17. Butler's Pantry
18. Dining Room
19. Entrance Hall & Staircase

EAST FRONT

NORTH FRONT

# The Story of the House

There can be hardly anyone, of whatever age or sex, who is not amused and intrigued by dolls' houses. They are naturally the special realm of little girls, but boys and even grown-up men and women are far from being immune to their fascination.

Almost everyone enjoys planning and arranging a full-size house, and the charm of a dolls' house lies in the fact that everything is crystallised into a small space, so that all the interest and beauty of design, decoration and arrangement can be taken in at a glance. More than this, while the beauties of a house are intensified by their concentration, the small defects and blemishes which are inseparable from seeing things life-size tend to disappear.

What must surely be the most complete and magnificent dolls' house in the world is Queen Mary's Dolls' House at Windsor Castle, where it is preserved in a large glass case arranged so that one may walk with ease all around it and see into all its rooms.

The suggestion for the creation of the House was first made in 1921, when a group of people conceived the desire to present to Her Majesty Queen Mary a gift that would serve as a token of national goodwill, and provide a means of raising funds for the many charitable schemes which Her Majesty had at heart. For this purpose the House was exhibited at the British Empire Exhibition at Wembley in 1924 and at the Ideal Home Exhibition in 1925.

In July 1925, the Dolls' House was brought to its present setting at Windsor, a room specially designed for it by the architect of the house, Sir Edwin Lutyens, from which it has never been moved. The Dolls' House is exhibited in special conditions to prevent deterioration from sunlight and atmospheric changes.

*LEFT: The monogram, worked in silk, on the canopy of Queen Mary's bed. The tiny, perfect stitches must have been remarkably difficult to work on the stiff damask fabric.*

*LEFT: Glass cabinets in the Queen's Sitting Room filled with jade and amber ornaments; the tiny animals include a water buffalo, a goat and a lion.*

*LEFT: A handsome Rudge motor-cycle and sidecar in British racing green with leather upholstery.*

*RIGHT: The Dolls' House being packed up in March 1924 ready to go on exhibition at Wembley.*

# The Building of the House

One important purpose in the minds of those who put forward the idea of Queen Mary's Dolls' House was to present a model of a house of the 20th century which should be fitted up with perfect fidelity, down to the smallest details, so as to represent as closely and minutely as possible a genuine and complete example of a domestic interior with all the household arrangements characteristic of the daily life of the time.

Such a purpose found a ready response in the heart of Queen Mary, who was one of the most home-loving of all our queens, and who had, herself, with great taste and knowledge, planned and supervised the redecoration and rearrangement of the rooms, furniture and works of art at Buckingham Palace and Windsor Castle.

Another and no less important aim was that the Dolls' House should give pleasure and be a source of gaiety, fantasy and wonder to people of all ages. No-one could have been found who summed up, in one personality, all that these various aims required more completely and successfully than Sir Edwin Lutyens. A scholarly yet original and enterprising architect, who built the new city of Delhi and the Cenotaph in Whitehall and who was the designer of many splendid English country houses, he was at the same time an intensely fun-loving person, and entered enthusiastically into the creation of the Dolls' House.

There is an extraordinary fascination and charm about smallness. Things cease to be as terrifying and unmanageable when they

are reduced in scale as they are in ordinary life, and there is a special satisfaction in creating a tiny replica of any object, whether it be a motor-car or a piece of furniture. In Queen Mary's Dolls' House the greatest care has been taken to make everything as closely as possible to the same scale of one-twelfth normal size, or one inch to the foot.

There are naturally a great many difficulties in making things to small proportions. A great number of quite unexpected problems also arise. Materials behave in a different way when used on a small scale. Fabrics such as clothing, bed-linen and table-cloths, although made of the finest and most delicate materials, seem to be unusually stiff, as anyone knows who has tried to dress a small doll, and who has found how difficult it is to get clothes to hang properly.

There are also special difficulties in making books to a very small scale, because leather, cloth and paper cannot be made one twelfth of their normal thickness. And the steel ropes

*ABOVE: The architect Sir Edwin Lutyens at work in his office. The Dolls' House absorbed him completely and no detail of the project escaped his attention. The house was constructed in the living room of his own house, depriving his family of its use for nearly two years.*

*RIGHT: A north-west view of the house showing its superbly dignified exterior painted to represent Portland stone. The house comprises over 40 rooms on four levels.*

which are used in lifts seem to become stiffer than ever when made on a small scale, and will not lie smoothly over the pulleys on which they work. For this reason the lift-ropes in Queen Mary's Dolls' House were made of fine fishing-line.

The door-locks throughout the house are marvels of ingenuity. For a full-size mansion of this character locks with eight levers would have been used, but such levers to proper scale would only have been of paper thickness, so three levers only are used, which is the normal number for an ordinary house. They all work with perfect smoothness and efficiency. The only difficulty is for a human being to turn the tiny keys.

A remarkable testimony of the accuracy and success with which all the objects in the various rooms have been made to scale is the fact that when we look at the photographs of the rooms we find it difficult to believe we are not looking at the rooms of a full-sized house, for hardly anything can be seen that jars on the eye by reason of its incorrect size. Down to the smallest detail of furnishing, accuracy of scale is maintained. In the principal rooms, the *Library, Saloon, Dining Room* and *State Bedrooms,* the illusion is perfect.

In its day Queen Mary's Dolls' House was extremely up-to-date in its equipment. It had electric light, a piped hot-water supply, an electric vacuum cleaner, an electric iron and many other labour-saving devices. The servants' rooms were far more comfortably equipped than was customary in most great houses of the time, and another innovation was the wood-block floor to the *Kitchen* which was actually said at the time to be adopted because a stone floor cut the hems of the servants' dresses!

Many of the articles in the Dolls' House, however, will never again be used or seen in a modern house and will even be some-

*RIGHT ABOVE:*
*Hot and cold water will flow through the shining taps in the Scullery. There are tiny bars of soap for washing up the gold-trimmed Doulton dishes and the copper saucepans.*

*RIGHT CENTRE:*
*A toy locomotive engine, its bell gleaming, halts at its destination on the Nursery floor. The engine is 4 inches (10 cm) long.*

*LEFT: The cricket bat was made by John Wisden & Co. Ltd and is shown here against a modern standard-size ball which measures 2¾ inches (7cm) in diameter. The house has a well-equipped games cupboard.*

*RIGHT: The two electric lifts have panelled interiors and glass doors – and electric lights of course. They are operated by the tiny press-buttons outside the lift-doors. The lifts are driven by an electric motor in the roof and the lift-ropes are made of fine fishing-line.*

*BELOW: The door-locks, including those on the furniture, are a feat of ingenuity and typical of the fine craftsmanship throughout the house.*

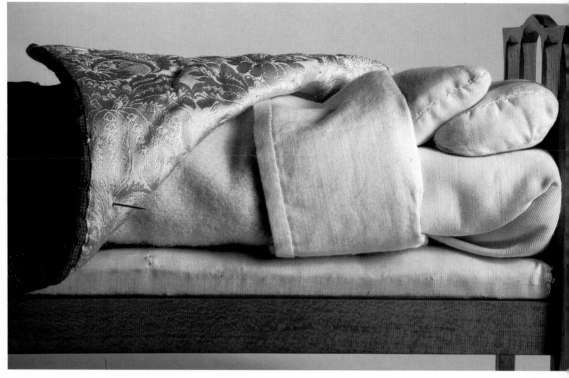

thing of a mystery to young people of today. There is, for example, the coal-burning kitchen range made of bright steel which had to be polished and have its flue swept of soot every day, and also the knife-polishing machine that was so necessary in the days before stainless steel came into use to keep the blades free of rust.

A reminder of the great revolution that has taken place in the treatment of illness is the provision in the *Nursery Suite* of '3 pneumonia jackets' in the days before penicillin and antibiotic drugs robbed this one-time dangerous disease of most of its terrors, and so we are able to see not only how a great house of the 1920s was decorated, furnished and arranged but also how every detail of life within its walls was organised and conducted.

*ABOVE: The butler's hardwood bed freshly made up with linen, woollen blanket and satin quilt. The mattress is made of horsehair.*

*BELOW: Monogrammed kitchen and table linen, bath towels, sheets, pillow-cases and blankets tied in different coloured ribbons according to its use.*

*BELOW RIGHT: The working treadle sewing-machine would keep the linen in good repair.*

*RIGHT AND FAR RIGHT: The house is unusually well-equipped for its day with modern comforts and labour-saving devices. It has electric lighting, an electric vacuum cleaner, electric iron, hot and cold running water in all five bathrooms and even flushing lavatories.*

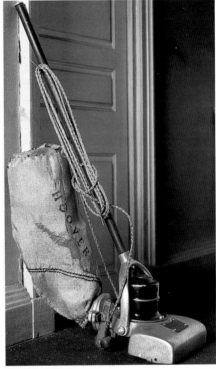

# *The Exterior of the House*

The Dolls' House building itself was designed to represent a great mansion in the classical tradition as it developed in England in the 17th and 18th centuries and was revived in the early years of the present century by Lutyens among other architects. It was in this tradition that most of the grand houses of England were built. The great delight of this model house is that we can appreciate at a single glance, as we could not do with a full-sized building of this kind, the satisfying proportions of the house and the perfect relationship of all the different parts one to the other.

Usually in dolls' houses the walls are fitted on hinges and regarded as doors, which are opened to reveal the rooms inside. With Queen Mary's Dolls' House it was desired that the interior should be seen without the very fine exterior being lost to sight, and this problem was solved by making the walls and roof in the form of an outer case which fits closely over the inner fabric and can be raised and lowered by electricity, rather like a lift.

The exterior is built of wood, painted to represent Portland stone, and the main façade is on the north front. It is highly dignified with its three levels of floors: the basement with its round-headed windows, the principal floor or *piano nobile*, and the attic. On the ground floor there are French casement doors, but all the others have sliding sashes, double hung with sash-lines and weights, and all opening smoothly.

The house stands on a base which is divided into two parts. The lower part, 24 inches (60cm) deep, contains 208 interchangeable drawers, each 11½ inches (29cm) long and 3½ (8cm) wide and deep, made of cedar. These were made for the storage of the population of dolls. The upper part of the base, 15 inches (38cm) deep, contains the machinery of the house, the electric transformers, the switches, the tank for bath waste, and the wine-cellar and store rooms for groceries, both of them amply and suitably victualled for a house of this size.

In this part of the base are also housed two surprising features. On the west side a flap falls down, a drawer extends, and there is a complete garage, with six model motor-cars and inspection pit in the painted brick paving, and all the work-benches, tools, equipment, and the petrol, oils and other supplies that such a garage would require. On the east side there is another flap which drops down to allow a beautiful and elaborate garden to be drawn forward on double runners.

*RIGHT:
The handsome east
front of the house.
The remarkable
garden was designed
by the famous English
gardener Gertrude
Jekyll. Its wrought-
iron gates open onto
a paved path, a green
velvet lawn and beds
of summer flowers.
The flowers, made of
various metals, were
each shaped by hand.*

*LEFT: Detail showing
the Royal coat of
arms set into the
classical pediment
on the north side of
the house. The main
façade is made more
impressive by six
Corinthian columns.*

We approach the house by the *west front* and first of all notice the *garage*, which has been opened out from a drawer in the base. The six motor-cars it contains are, like many things in Queen Mary's Dolls' House, of even greater interest today than when first made in the 1920s, for these are now valuable antiques of the motor world, the vintage cars which are now so eagerly sought after by enthusiasts. They consist of a Rolls-Royce Silver Ghost 7-seater limousine-landaulet; a 40 h.p. Daimler with a Barker body; a Daimler shooting-brake; a Lanchester 7-seater saloon; a 14/40 h.p. Vauxhall saloon; and a Sunbeam open tourer. There are also a Rudge motor-cycle and sidecar, a fire-engine, two perambulators and a bicycle.

The *north front* has its centre portion made more impressive by a slight projection, and by six Corinthian columns surmounted by a pediment containing the Royal Arms. The *attic storey* is crowned with a balustrade which carries a number of statues and vases in lead, the work of Sir George Frampton RA. The figures at the four corners represent the patron saints of England, Scotland, Wales and Ireland. In the centre of the parapet is an angel bearing the Queen's crown, and the four remaining figures are emblematic of Queen Mary's Christian names, Mary, Louise, Victoria and Augusta.

With the whole of the main façade open to us, we see at a single glance what cannot so quickly and easily be grasped in a full-sized mansion, how the internal planning of the house reflects the external design, with the grand staircase hall corresponding to the central portion of the front, and rising through three storeys, flanked by lobbies that communicate with the various rooms of the house. As in so many great English mansions, there is a *lower hall* with an entry from the grounds. From here, flanked by a wrought-iron balustrade in the style of Louis XIV, designed and presented by Mr Starkie Gardner, the marble stairs rise to the *main hall* above, which is formed in the classic proportion of a cube, and with a deeply coved ceiling. The walls reflect a somewhat solemn theme, that of 'The Expulsion of Adam and Eve from Paradise', painted by Sir William Nicholson.

In the circular niches are busts of Earls Haig and

Beatty by C. S. Jagger and on marble pedestals below are busts of King Edward VII and Queen Alexandra by Sir W. Goscombe John.

Behind the glass doors in the lobbies to the right runs the *lift shaft*, with two lifts driven by an electric motor in the roof. They are operated by tiny press-buttons outside the lift-doors, since these are too small for us to enter. On the mezzanine floor to the left is a *Servant's Bedroom* and above it a *Housemaid's Closet*.

On the *east front* of the house, where it will catch the sunlight of the early morning, is the *garden*, which was planned by one of the greatest of all English gardeners, Gertrude Jekyll. When it was decided to make the garden capable of being stored in one of the drawers of the base, it was obvious that the problems of design and construction would be difficult, but they have been ingeniously

*LEFT: The close-fitting outer shell of the house lifts up to reveal the tantalising interior. The outer shell can be raised or lowered by machinery installed in the roof space.*

*RIGHT: A garden spade and fork rest against the garden wall.*

*BELOW: A tiny baby carriage, one of two to be found in the garden, each 3½ inches (9 cm) long.*

overcome by fixing the trees inside the front of the drawer so that they lie horizontally, just clearing the tops of the garden flowers, when the drawer is closed.

The iron gates and the balustrade, which returns a little way back on both sides, are also fixed to the drawer front, which is invisibly hinged at the back line of the front paving where it comes next to the grass. The grass is of green velvet, and is shorn in imagination by the Atco motor mowing machine, which is exactly to scale. On each side of the paved central path are two groups of four flower-beds, planted with clumps of blue and purple irises, with a standard rose at each angle, and a filling of summer flowers – lilies and orange tiger-lilies, carnations, sweet peas, poppies, marigolds, gentians and fuchsias.

Round Italian terracotta pots hold agapanthus, and various flowers are growing in troughs which may be moved about the garden as one pleases. In wooden tubs are hydrangeas and rhododendrons. Oak garden seats stand on the paths. The two side walks have magnolia grandiflora trained against the masonry. Climbing roses trail delightfully over the niches of the back wall; they are kept rather pale in colour in accordance with Gertrude Jekyll's principles of design so that they may not compete with the brighter flowers of the middle garden.

The gardeners cannot have been about today, for on the path to the left a fairy-ring of toadstools has sprung up overnight. A very close search will reveal some snails, and even some eggs in a thrush's nest. Some butterflies have settled upon the flowers, and birds are resting on the trees. The flowers were made of various kinds of metals, and every one of the petals and leaves has been bent to shape by a patient hand.

# *The Library*

The most important room on the *west front* is the *Library*, a handsome room panelled from floor to cornice in Italian walnut, with deeply recessed bookcases, and screened at the ends by Ionic columns of the same wood. The ceiling has a fluted coving and is painted in a Palladian design by William Walcot. The marble fireplace is again convincingly of early Georgian character. The 'Tudor' portraits are of King Henry VII, King Henry VIII and Queen Elizabeth I.

The *Library* contains two collections which are among the greatest miracles of the whole house. The first of these is the collection of prints, watercolours and drawings, over seven hundred of them, some of which are stored in two large walnut cabinets in the manner adopted by collectors who lived in the great houses of the past. Many artists' names are still famous today, including Oswald Birley, Laura Knight, William Orpen, Russell Flint, Edmund Dulac, Sir William Nicholson, John Nash, Paul Nash, and Mark Gertler. Others, celebrated in their day, are now less well-known. Taken all together, they provide a good cross-section of artistic life in England in the early years of the century.

No artists ever convey the essential spirit of a period so vividly as do the caricaturists and cartoonists. Here among the pictures is a fascinating group of amusing drawings by the best comic artists of the 1920s Tom Webster, George Morrow, George Belcher, Lewis Baumer, H. M. Bateman, W. K. Haselden, W. Heath Robinson, G. E. Studdy, 'Poy', Will Owen and 'Fougasse'. The names conjure up a nostalgic picture of the carefree days between the two great wars.

The collection of books is, if possible, even more remarkable. The majority of them were specially written by their respective authors for the Dolls' House, many of them in the author's own handwriting. They form a remarkable survey of English literature in the

1920s. Perhaps some of the most interesting books are those contributed by the poets, and here are tiny volumes containing verses by Edmund Blunden, Robert Bridges, Hilaire Belloc, G. K. Chesterton, W. H. Davies, Walter de la Mare, Robert Graves, A. E. Housman, Thomas Hardy, Rudyard Kipling, Henry Newbolt, Siegfried Sassoon and many others.

Among other writers represented are Max Beerbohm, Arnold Bennett, Joseph Conrad, Arthur Conan Doyle, John Galsworthy, Aldous Huxley and W. Somerset Maugham. The *Library* also contains a number of Bibles and a Koran, the complete works of Shakespeare, a volume of Charles

RIGHT: A corner of the Library showing the magnificent globe and the gun cupboard against the wall. The pair of Purdey shotguns in the gun cupboard are normally displayed on a cabinet in the main part of the Library. Purdey's continue to be gunmakers to the Royal Family today.

LEFT: The exquisite hand-tooled leather bookbindings are evidence of extraordinary craftsmanship. Arthur Conan Doyle, W. Somerset Maugham and Rudyard Kipling are among many famous names on the Library shelves. Most of the books were specially written by their respective authors for the Dolls' House.

Dickens and all the standard reference books.

A special reminder of the unusual responsibilities of the inhabitants of a house like this is given by the presence on another desk of a group of the official despatch boxes, covered in red, dark blue and dark green morocco, that come from the various government departments with urgent and important messages demanding attention at all hours of the day and night. The bindings of many of the tiny books are exquisite gems of craftsmanship, in scarlet, blue, green and purple leather, and microscopically ornamented with delicate gold tooling.

*BELOW LEFT: Stamp album donated by Stanley Gibbons, containing facsimiles of English and Colonial stamps. King George V was an enthusiastic stamp collector.*

*BELOW RIGHT: The columns, bookshelves, panelling and furniture in the Library are of Italian walnut. The two cabinets contain the large collection of miniature pictures, (DETAIL, BOTTOM LEFT), many by well-known artists such as Russell Flint and Paul Nash. Upon the right-hand cabinet sit the official despatch boxes with urgent messages for the owner of the house. Above the marble fireplace hangs Sir William Nicholson's portrait of Queen Elizabeth I.*

Lady Patricia Ramsay.
[H.R.H. Princess Patricia of Connaught.]

Dora Webb, A.R.M.S.

*FAR LEFT: Still life by Lady Patricia Ramsay, first cousin of King George V, and (LEFT), a drawing of King Edward VIII as a young cadet by Dora Webb, two of the 700 drawings stored in the Dolls' House.*

# *The King's Bedroom*

The *King's Bedroom* is a soberly magnificent apartment rising the full height of the *piano nobile*, or main storey. Here the deeply coved ceiling has been painted by George Plank with a delightful design representing a garden pergola with its trellis made in the form of a musical stave, on which the notes are roses arranged as the score of the National Anthem.

The fireplace is of white basalt, and yellow marble, and above it hangs Ambrose McEvoy's portrait of Princess Mary. The walls are painted as oriental hangings, also by George Plank.

In the arched lobby to the left of the Bedroom is the *King's Wardrobe*, its groined ceiling painted by William de Glehn. There are exquisitely panelled and white-painted woodwork cupboards and a ceremonial sword lies on a round table in the centre of the wardrobe. On the opposite side in another lobby is the *King's Bathroom*, the ceiling here painted by Laurence Irving, and the floor of white marble with a bath of green African Verdite marble.

On the upper mezzanine floor above the lobbies of the *King's Bedroom* are two neatly furnished *servants' bedrooms*. Above to the left on the *Nursery Floor* is the *Princess Royal's Room*, with a mahogany four-poster bed with cane panels designed by Sir Edwin Lutyens himself.

A connecting door leads to the *Queen's Sitting-Room*, a delightfully golden-coloured room decorated and furnished in the oriental spirit that Queen Mary loved. The walls are painted with clouds and foliage by Edmund Dulac, while the bamboo-pattern chairs and the lacquer desk are painted a cool yellow.

A Chinese rug, a tiny carved screen of Coromandel lacquer and minute ornaments of Chinese porcelain and jade complete the oriental furnishings.

Beyond is the *Night Nursery*, containing a beautiful mahogany 'Chippendale' four-poster bed (for the nanny), and one of the most remarkable pieces of furniture in the whole house – a tiny cradle of unpolished apple-wood, inlaid and bound with silver, the interior lined with ivory, with the Prince of Wales's feathers on the hood. *The Nursery Bathroom* is the last room to be seen on this floor. The bathroom is simple yet well-equipped, with hard flooring, a porcelain bath and washstand and a painted wooden chair.

*OPPOSITE ABOVE: The King's Bedroom. The State Bed has red and gold silk damask hangings embroidered with the Royal Arms. The furniture is 'Queen Anne' and 'Chippendale'.*

*OPPOSITE BELOW: The Queen's Sitting-Room. The room is decorated in the oriental style, the furniture lacquered cream and gold.*

*ABOVE: The King's Bathroom is sumptuously decorated, with a white marble floor, green marble bath, recess, wash-basin surrounds and wall-panelling, and silver taps.*

# *The Dining Room*

The *Dining Room*, on the ground floor of the *east front*, is an extremely handsome panelled room in late 17th- or early 18th-century style with a ceiling of Palladian design, the panels of which are painted by Gerald Moira with lively figures in richly coloured landscapes. The wide mouldings of the ceiling are repeated in the pattern of the carpet below, which was painted by Ernest Thesiger in imitation of an Aubusson carpet. The walls are painted grey, and are decorated in the manner of Grinling Gibbons with pendants of flowers and fruit carved in limewood picked out with gold.

The extending dining-table in the centre measures 5½ inches (13cm) when closed and 20 inches (50cm) when open, with mechanism of perfect construction. The accompanying chairs are remarkable in their accuracy of detail. They are of walnut and covered with red leather.

Over the marble fireplace hangs a painting of HRH the Prince of Wales (later King Edward VIII) by the artist A. J. Munnings. Two smaller paintings by the same artist hang at the sides, below large portraits of King Edward III to the left and King James V of Scotland to the right, by William Llewellyn.

At one end of the room hangs a copy by Ambrose McEvoy of Winterhalter's famous painting of Queen Victoria, Prince Albert and children which hangs at Buckingham Palace and two views of the State Apartments at Windsor. Facing it at the other end is a large flower and still-life composition by W. B. E. Ranken and two small pictures of the Coronation of George V and Queen Mary by Captain Pearse.

Immediately adjoining the *Dining Room*, to the left, is the *Butler's Pantry*, with its white-painted cupboard for china and glassware, and a double sink. A coffee-pot and some other exquisitely made articles of silver stand on one side. Above the *Pantry* is the *Strong Room*, where the magnificent Crown Jewels in tiny replica are appropriately protected by a steel grille.

OPPOSITE BELOW: *The Dining Room. The table is laid with silver and glass for 14 places and there is even tiny fruit on the porcelain dessert dishes. The walnut chairs have red leather seats, arms carved with eagles' heads and legs with claw and ball feet. There are also three walnut side-tables with marble tops, legs carved and gilded with lion-paw feet.*

LEFT: *There are five silver candelabra in the Dining Room. The candles are kept in the cellars. Both the gold plate and the silver would have been fetched by the butler from the Strong Room.*

BELOW LEFT: *The Strong Room. Behind the steel grilles are kept the Crown Jewels as well as the silver-gilt dinner service for 18 people made by Garrard, the Crown jewellers.*

BELOW: *The painting of Queen Victoria and Prince Albert and their children is by McEvoy after Winterhalter.*

# *The Saloon*

Extending across the full width of the principal floor on the *east front* is the largest, grandest and most elaborately furnished room in Queen Mary's Dolls' House. This is the *Saloon*, which is intended both as a Throne Room and as a withdrawing-room for the Royal Lady and her guests. The panels of the ceiling are painted by Charles Sims, with misty, scarlet-winged figures, and the high coving is decorated with a lozenge design and with figures of nymphs.

The chimney-piece of the *Saloon* is a magnificent feature with handsome columns and

a pediment in various marbles. Above the fireplace is a portrait of the Electress Sophia, ancestress of the Royal Family, by A. S. Cope, and flanking it on the rose damask-covered walls are State portraits of King George V and Queen Mary in their Coronation robes by William Orpen.

The silk wall-covering, which provides such a sumptuous background to pictures and furniture, is woven to a pattern of the days of Queen Anne, to the incredibly small scale of 120 threads to an inch.

From this scene of regal splendour we ascend to the upper regions, where is centred the domestic organisation that keeps the whole of this great house working smoothly. In the centre of the top floor on this front is the *Linen Room*, which contains a remarkable stock of tiny linen, all of it specially hand-woven in Ireland, and each item microscopically stitched in the corner with the Royal monogram by a Franco-Irish lady who devoted 1,500 hours of her life to this task. There is a tiny treadle sewing-machine.

Adjoining the *Linen Room* on one side is the *Housekeeper's Room* and on the other her private *bathroom*, both of them comfortably equipped.

OPPOSITE ABOVE: *The Saloon. Extending across the full width of the east front, this room is large and grand. In addition to its use as a drawing-room it serves as the Throne Room for ceremonial occasions. The State portraits of King George V and Queen Mary are by William Orpen.*

OPPOSITE BELOW: *The Linen Room. Tiny wickerwork laundry baskets with leather fastenings are among many marvellous miniature objects in this room.*

ABOVE LEFT: *The grand piano was designed by Lutyens and made by John Broadwood and Sons Ltd.*

FAR LEFT: *The King's and Queen's silver thrones, appropriately adorned, await their occupants.*

LEFT: *Detail of pedestal clock in a walnut case, one of a pair in the Saloon.*

# The Queen's Bedroom

The *Queen's Bedroom* on the *south front* is one of the most splendid apartments of the House. The high coved ceiling is painted by Glyn Philpot, representing Day and Night. Round the cove are great masses of dark night-clouds lit with gold by the setting sun, while in the flat ceiling panel we see as through a sky-light the small white fleecy clouds and tranquil blue sky of morning.

The stately canopy bed is hung with silk damask of the same restful blue-grey as that which covers the walls.

The quilted bed-cover, of the same colour, is woven with a diamond pattern enhanced by a tiny seed-pearl at each corner. The carpet is astonishingly beautiful, of tapestry-work in a French Aubusson design, the threads from which were specially hand-spun, dyed and woven. It measures 13¾ in (35cm) by 16½ in (42cm).

To the left on the same floor is a room which will be, for many people, the most astonishing room of all, the *Queen's Bathroom*. Here the walls are painted ivory, with

*OPPOSITE BELOW: The Queen's Bedroom.*

*OPPOSITE BELOW: The Queen's Bedroom. The walls and the bed are hung with blue-grey damask silk, and above the fireplace hangs a portrait of Queen Mary's mother, the Duchess of Teck, by F. O. Salisbury. The room contains some of the most exquisitely made pieces of furniture in the whole house. There is the dressing-table made of wood, painted to look like pleated silk; the walnut writing table with its tiny handles to the drawers; the gilt day-bed, and the wardrobe of amboyna wood, with its lock and key that work perfectly.*

*RIGHT: The Queen's Bathroom. This astonishing room has an alabaster bath with silver taps, a mother-of-pearl floor and a ceiling painted with mermaids.*

*BELOW RIGHT: A miniature bonsai tree and jade animals adorn a side table in the Queen's Bedroom.*

panels of shagreen, and a mother-of-pearl floor. The vaulted ceiling is painted by Maurice Grieffenhagen, with figures of mermaids. The bath and washstand are of alabaster, with silver taps, which can be made, if not actually to run, at least to drip with water, for the circulation is very slow through the tiny pipes.

In one of the niches is a beautifully made satinwood chest of drawers with a bow-front in the Hepplewhite style. On the *Mezzanine* floor above the *Queen's Bedroom* are a *Servant's Room* to the right, and to the left the *Trunk-Room*, with an astonishing collection of minute trunks, hatboxes and cases, all made with remarkable accuracy.

# The Kitchen & Scullery

The *Kitchen* is a high room, for the sake of coolness and good ventilation, and the walls are tiled for ease of cleaning. Here, possibly more than anywhere else in the house, we realise how greatly our domestic arrangements have changed in the twentieth century.

The floor is made of 2,500 tiny wood-blocks, with a strip of slate-flooring in front of the cooking range, hotplate and pastry oven which are all placed along one wall. Every detail of the range and cupboards is perfectly carried out with hinges and handles in shining bright steel. They are designed to use not gas or electricity but coal, so the flues would have had to be swept every day.

*ABOVE AND LEFT: The Kitchen. The equipment is remarkably complete and accurate in scale, including, as well as its own china service and copper cooking utensils, tiny cutlery, a mincing machine, weighing machine and a coffee-mill that works.*

*RIGHT: The Wine Cellar. The cellar was stocked by wine merchants Berry Bros. & Co. (still Royal Warrant holders today). As well as wines of famous vintage, there are gin, whisky and beer in casks and in bottles.*

*LEFT: The bottles in the Wine Cellar are only an inch (2.5cm) high. This one stands on top of a normal-sized cork. The corks in the miniature bottles were tight but after 60 years some evaporation has occurred.*

*BELOW RIGHT: Bass beer, stored in bottles and barrels, made good refreshment for the servants.*

Adjoining to the left is the *Scullery*, with deep, lead-lined sinks in which real hot and cold water can flow from the shining taps. Above them is a tiny plate-rack, and nearby is a vegetable bin, with mops and dish-cloths, scrubbing brushes and minute bars of soap.

In the *Wine Cellar* are still preserved some of the finest vintages of the time when the house was built, including 1906 champagne, 1875 claret and 1854 brandy. As well as wine there are beers and whisky, both in casks, and a plentiful supply of liqueurs and soft drinks.

# *The Day Nursery*

The *Day Nursery* is a delightful spacious room, the walls painted by Edmund Dulac with paintings of fairytales in oriental style. The Chinese Emperor's daughter receives the salutations of some fat mandarins as she steps from her pagoda; Cinderella is seen riding in her coach; Sinbad the Sailor waves from his boat to Robinson Crusoe on his island; Ali Baba drives his laden asses past Bluebeard's castle, while Puss-in-Boots and the Frog Prince pay their respects to a fair Princess; and last of all there are brave Jack on his Beanstalk and little Red Riding Hood being waylaid by the Wolf.

Our tour of Queen Mary's Dolls' House is over, and we must prepare to enter the everyday world again. We have done more than visit a realm of childhood enchantment; we have seen in miniature a great English mansion of the kind where in the past the arts of architecture, of decoration, of fine furniture-making, of silver-work, of painting, music and literature, of tapestry and carpet-weaving, of bookbinding and a host of other arts and crafts were purposefully fostered.

Here we have seen the great English House as it was shaped by tradition and creative inspiration at the stage it had reached in the second decade of the twentieth century, and we have seen something of the highly developed domestic organisation upon which a house like this depended for its running and maintenance.

The creation of a full-sized house such as this with all its treasures was in the past the result of the pursuit of perfection in a hundred different fields by the host of architects, designers, artists, writers, musicians, craftsmen and other hard-working people who made their different contributions to its realisation. In the making of this house in miniature this search for perfection has been intensified a hundredfold, and is the object of our special admiration.

No other house will ever be built in this fashion again, and so Queen Mary's Dolls' House, as well as being a wonderful toy and, as it were, a domestic museum, is also a social document of the time of Queen Mary, who inspired its creation.

*RIGHT: The Day Nursery. Decorated with scenes from fairytales, the nursery has amongst its treasures a toy theatre, a wind-up gramophone, a set of toy soldiers and a toy train.*

*BELOW: The brightly painted wooden toys contribute to the enchanting childhood world created in the Day Nursery.*